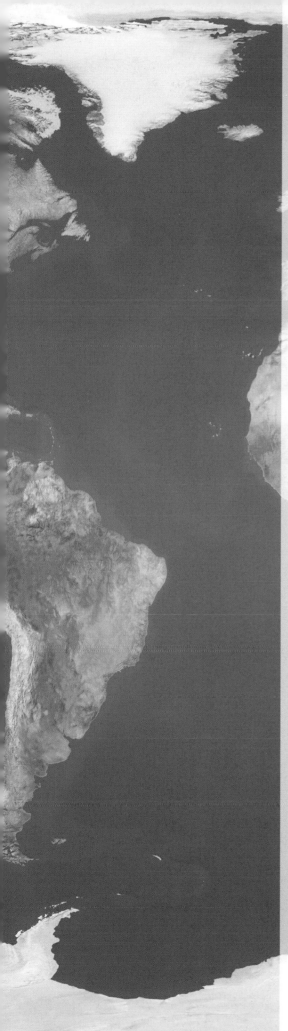

Contents

Biomes of the world

Biologists divide the living world into major zones called biomes. Each biome has its own distinctive climate, plants and animals.

If you were to walk all the way from the north of Canada to the Amazon **rainforest**, you'd notice the wilderness changing dramatically along the way.

Northern Canada is a freezing and barren place without trees, where only tiny brownish-green plants can survive in the icy ground. But trudge south for long enough and you enter a magical world of **conifer** forests, where moose, caribou (reindeer) and wolves live. After several weeks, the conifers disappear, and you reach the grass-covered prairies of the central USA. The further south you go, the drier the land gets and the hotter the sun feels, until you find yourself hiking through a cactus-filled **desert**. But once you reach southern Mexico, the cacti start to disappear, and strange **tropical** trees begin to take their place. Here, the muggy air is filled with the calls of exotic birds and the drone of tropical insects. Finally, in Colombia you cross the Andes mountain range – whose chilly peaks remind you a little of your starting point – and descend into the dense, swampy jungles of the Amazon rainforest.

Desert is the driest biome. There are hot deserts and cold ones.

Taiga is made up of conifer trees that can survive freezing winters.

Scientists have a special name for the different regions – such as desert, tropical rainforest and prairie – that you'd pass through on such a journey. They call them **biomes**. Everywhere on Earth can be classified as being in one biome or another, and the same biome often appears in lots of

Biomes Atlases

TAIGA

Trevor Day

Raintree

www.raintreepublishers.co.uk

 Phone 44 (0) 1865 888112
Send a fax to 44 (0) 1865 314091
Visit the Raintree bookshop online at www.raintreepublishers.co.uk
to browse our catalogue and order online.

First published in Great Britain in 2003 by Raintree, Halley Court,
Jordan Hill, Oxford, OX2 8EJ, part of Harcourt Education Ltd.
Raintree is a registered trademark of Harcourt Education Ltd.
Copyright © 2003 The Brown Reference Group plc.
First published in paperback in 2004.
The moral right of the proprieter has been asserted.

Printed and bound in Singapore.

ISBN 1 844 21155 X (hardback)   ISBN 1 844 21169 X (paperback)
07 06 05 04 03   08 07 06 05 04
10 9 8 7 6 5 4 3 2 1   10 9 8 7 6 5 4 3 2 1

British Library Cataloging-in-Publication Data

A full catalogue is available for this book from the British Library.

The Brown Reference Group plc
Project Editor: Ben Morgan
Deputy Editor: Dr. Rob Houston
Copy-editors: John Farndon and Angela Koo
Consultant: Dr. Mark Hostetler, Department
    of Wildlife Ecology and Conservation,
    University of Florida
Designer: Reg Cox
Cartographers: Mark Walker and
    Darren Awuah
Picture Researcher: Clare Newman
Indexer: Kay Ollerenshaw
Managing Editor: Bridget Giles
Design Manager: Lynne Ross
Production: Alastair Gourlay

Raintree Publishers
Editors: Isabel Thomas and Kate Buckingham

Front cover: Giant redwoods,
north-western USA.
Inset: Grey wolves.

Title page: Moose.

The acknowledgments on p. 64 form
part of this copyright page. Every effort has
been made to contact copyright holders of
any material reproduced in this book. Any
omissions will be rectified in subsequent
printings if notice is given to the publishers.

About this book

This book's introductory pages describe the biomes of the world and then the taiga biome. The five main chapters look at aspects of the taiga: climate, plants, animals, people and future. Between the chapters are detailed maps that focus on key taiga regions. The map pages are shown in the contents in italics, *like this*.

Throughout the book you'll also find boxed stories or fact files about the taiga. The icons here show what the boxes are about. At the end of the book is a glossary, which explains all the difficult words. After that is a list of books and websites for further research and an index, allowing you to locate subjects anywhere in the book.

 Climate

 People

 Plants

 Future

 Animals

 Facts

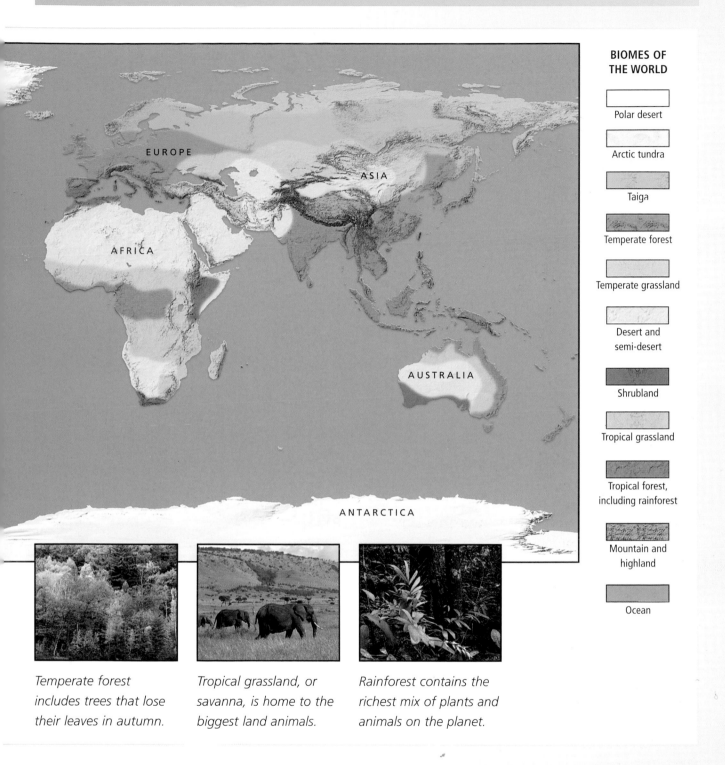

BIOMES OF THE WORLD

Polar desert

Arctic tundra

Taiga

Temperate forest

Temperate grassland

Desert and semi-desert

Shrubland

Tropical grassland

Tropical forest, including rainforest

Mountain and highland

Ocean

Temperate forest includes trees that lose their leaves in autumn.

Tropical grassland, or savanna, is home to the biggest land animals.

Rainforest contains the richest mix of plants and animals on the planet.

different places. For instance, there are areas of rainforest as far apart as Brazil, Africa and South-east Asia. Although the plants and animals that inhabit these forests are different, they live in similar ways. Likewise, the prairies of North America are part of the grassland biome, which also occurs in China, Australia and Argentina. Wherever there are grasslands, there are grazing animals that feed on the grass, as well as large carnivores that hunt and kill the grazers.

The map on this page shows how the world's major biomes fit together to make up the biosphere – the zone of life on Earth.

The taiga biome

Taiga forests occupy a larger area than all the tropical rainforests. They grow in a region of extreme weather encircling the northern hemisphere from Alaska to Japan.

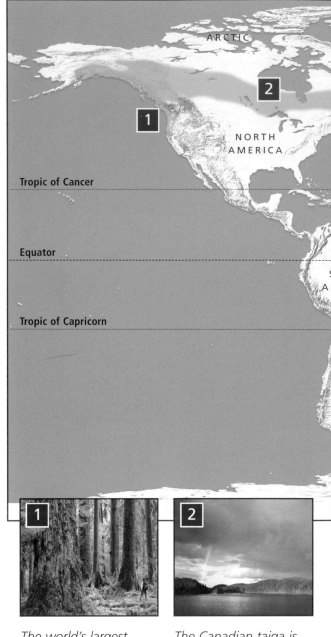

The world's largest trees grow in forests on the Pacific coast.

The Canadian taiga is dotted with thousands of beautiful lakes.

Taiga occupies about one-tenth of the Earth's land surface, and as a land biome it is second in size only to deserts. The forests that grow in the taiga biome are filled with mainly conifer trees. Conifer trees keep their leaves all year round and produce cones rather than flowers. Often, only two or three conifer **species**, such as spruces, pines or firs, cover large areas of the forest.

Most of the taiga grows in icy land near the Arctic Circle – the coldest place in which full-size trees can grow. This sort of taiga is called boreal forest. Some taiga forest grows along the north-west coast of North America. There is so much rainfall there that the taiga is described as rainforest. Despite this name, these forests are filled mainly with conifers and are more similar to boreal forests than to the tropical rainforests around the **equator**.

The word *taiga* comes from the Russian word for 'marshy pine forest', which is a very apt description. Boreal forest is named for *Boreas*, the Greek god of the north wind.

Beyond the northern limit of taiga, the temperatures are too low for full-size trees to grow, and **tundra** – a biome with plants no larger than shrubs – replaces taiga. At its southern limit, taiga gives way to forests of broad-leaved trees and **temperate** grasslands. In between, vast areas of the taiga form dense, almost impenetrable forest. However, the landscape sometimes creates a jigsaw puzzle of forests, wetlands and lakes.

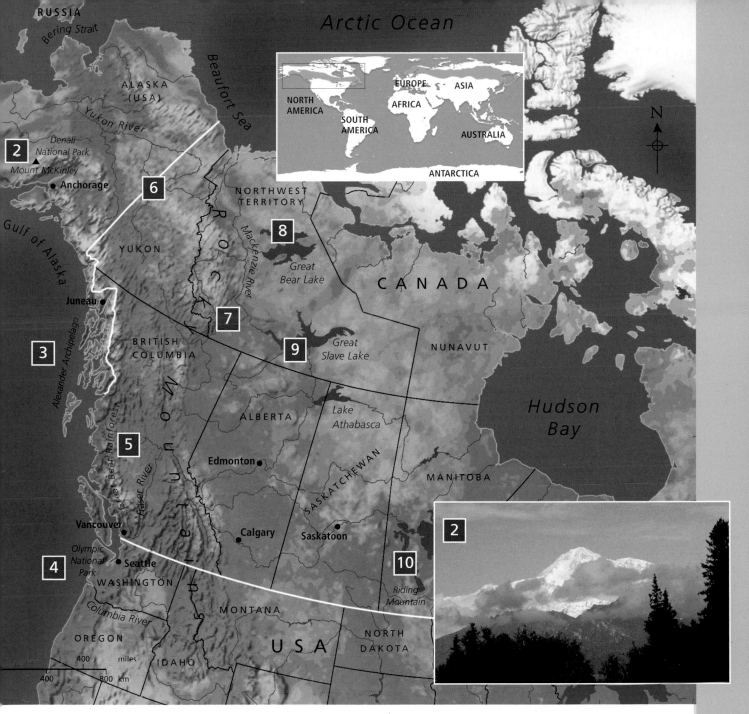

1. Kodiak Island
The first European colony in Alaska was on this island, when Russian settlers arrived in 1784. Brown bears are common.

2. Denali National Park and Mount McKinley
The world's second-largest taiga reserve includes Mount McKinley, the tallest point in North America at 6194 metres (20,320 ft).

3. Alexander Archipelago
A group of islands that are home to Alaska's Haida people.

4. Olympic National Park
Luxuriant mountain rainforest on the coast of Washington.

5. Great Bear Rainforest
The largest of North America's Pacific rainforests. It is home to 2000 grizzly bears and contains trees that are 1000 years old.

6. Yukon
A remote area of mountains, forests and plateaus, named after one of Canada's longest rivers. The site of the 1896 Klondike gold strike.

7. Rocky Mountains
The Rockies run nearly 4800 km (3000 miles) from Alaska in the north to Mexico in the south.

8. Great Bear Lake
Canada's largest lake is at the northern fringe of the taiga.

9. Mackenzie River and Great Slave Lake
Canada's longest river flows from the Great Slave Lake to the Arctic Ocean. Much of the river is over 1.6 km (1 mile) wide.

10. Riding Mountain National Park
An island of taiga surrounded by temperate grassland.

Taiga climate

For most of the year, taiga is dark, cold and covered in snow and ice. During the short periods of warmth in spring and summer, the days get longer, the ice and snow melt and the forest comes to life.

The climate of taiga forest is very harsh, with snow and ice covering the ground for much of the year. The plant life is shrouded in water, but this water is in a frozen form that plants cannot use. During the long winter, plants endure a water shortage as severe as that in deserts. However, with the spring thaw, the reverse is true, and there is an abundance of liquid water. Now, plants have to cope with soils that are very damp or have had all the **nutrients** washed out of them. Despite all these difficulties, conifer trees thrive in taiga forests.

Around the world
As with other land biomes, taiga exists because the particular combination of **climate** and soil favours certain kinds of plants. The long, cool winters and short, warm summers of this biome occur in lowlands in the far

A thick layer of snow weighs down conifer trees in a foggy forest in Norway. Taiga forests are covered in snow for most of the year.

north of North America, Europe and Asia. Similar conditions also exist further south on the slopes of tall mountains, and taiga-like forests grow there, too. No taiga forest grows in the southern **hemisphere**. This is because the area where taiga would grow is mainly covered by ocean.

Taiga develops where the growing season for plants is at least three months, and where the average daily temperature in the warmest month of the year is about 10°C (50°F). In winter, temperatures in some taiga forests can be even lower than in the Arctic tundra to the north. In fact, northern Siberia is one of the coldest places on Earth – chillier than anywhere, except for Antarctica. In much of Siberia, differences between summer and winter temperatures are also among the largest anywhere. In winter, temperatures can plunge to as low as −68°C (−90°F), while in summer they soar to 30°C (86°F) – a temperature range approaching a phenomenal 100°C (180°F).

The taiga may be cold for much of the year, but the presence of snow can benefit plants. Snow acts like a fluffy, air-filled jacket, insulating trees and soil from the bitterly cold air. In winter, the soil at a depth of 50 cm (20 in) can be 20°C (36°F) warmer than the air above. At these depths, tree roots are still able to take in life-giving water, even though the temperatures above ground are well below freezing.

Hardy trees

Conifers dominate the taiga. Few broad-leaved, **deciduous** trees, which shed their leaves each year, survive in the biome. Because taiga areas have such short growing seasons, deciduous trees are at a disadvantage.

Right: Needles of a white pine tree dripping with meltwater. When the snow and ice melt, taiga forests become very wet indeed.

Mountainside forests

Well beyond the southern limit of lowland boreal taiga, conifer forests grow on mountain slopes where temperatures are much cooler than surrounding low-lying areas. The trees in these high-altitude (high above sea level) forests are very similar to those that live in areas of boreal taiga. For example, the highland forests of the Alps and Pyrenees mountains in Europe contain the same species of pine and fir tree that grow in the taiga forests in the far north of Europe.

The Earth is warmer near the equator than at the poles. Therefore, as a rule, the mountains that are nearer the equator, and further from true taiga, have taiga-like conditions higher up and are home to more non-taiga trees. Near the northern end of the Rocky Mountains in North America (below), conifer forests grow to a treeline (the upper limit of tree growth) at an altitude of only 1500 metres (4900 ft). In the warmer, more southerly Rockies of Colorado, the belt of conifer forest begins at an altitude of about 2130 metres (6900 ft) and the treeline reaches to about 3200 metres (9900 ft) above sea level.

Plants **photosynthesize** (make food from sunlight) with their leaves. Each spring, deciduous trees must grow a new set of leaves, which they then shed when the weather gets cooler in the autumn. This is very wasteful if the growing season is only short. Coniferous evergreens keep their needle-like leaves for several years. They are, therefore, ready to photosynthesize and grow as soon as spring begins.

Humid summers

The conifer trees of the taiga are well suited to coping with cold and dampness, but they cannot tolerate warmth coupled with dryness. When plant enthusiasts grow taiga trees in botanical gardens and give them plenty of water in summer, the trees still fare poorly if the air is dry. They lose water through their needles and grow to only a fraction of the size they would reach in their normal habitat. Spruces cultivated in warm climates grow to half their natural height.

Waterlogged soil

The layered soil of taiga forest is called podzol, from the Russian word for ash, which describes the colour of one of the soil's layers. Podzol forms because taiga climates are so cold, and because the pine needles shed by conifers are broken down very slowly by decomposers in the soil. As a result, the ground becomes covered in a thick layer of pine needles and other debris shed by trees. These layers eventually form podzol.

The combination of cold and wet conditions, plus slowly decaying plant matter, makes the upper region of the soil acidic. Over the year, the amount of water falling as snow, rain or hail is much greater than that rising into the air by **evaporation**. The extra water sinks into the ground and is turned acidic by the soil. This acid-rich

In the short summer, taiga forest is bathed in warm sunshine during very long days. At the northern limit of the taiga, the sun sets for only a few hours a day.

The world's largest trees

On North America's Pacific coast, running from Alaska and Canada in the north to California in the south, coniferous forests clothe the western mountain ranges. Here, winters are milder and wetter than in other northern forests, but the plant life is similar to boreal taiga: pine, fir, spruce, hemlock and larch.

The forests receive an enormous amount of rain – over 4 metres (13 ft) every year, and they are called rainforests because of this. The coastal mountains trap the wind blowing in from the ocean, and this moist wind releases its rain as it rises up the mountainside. The western slopes get all the rain, while the region to the east of the mountains is much drier.

The mountains also protect the rainforests from the icy air that travels down from the Arctic. On the coast, the temperature rarely drops below freezing, while on the eastern side of the mountains, the forests must cope with much colder weather.

Being so wet, the forests have an almost tropical luxuriance, with an undergrowth of ferns, and thick mosses and lichens. In north California and south-west Oregon, the forests are infiltrated by giant redwoods (above), the largest trees on Earth. The Redwood National Park of northern California is home to the biggest tree in the world – a 112-metre (367-ft) coast redwood, which has bark 30 cm (1 ft) thick.

Climographs

Each place in the world has its own pattern of weather. The typical pattern of weather that happens in one place during a year is called climate. We can sum up a place's climate on a climograph, such as the one shown here for St Louis in the USA. The letters along the bottom are the months of the year. The numbers on the left and the small bars show rainfall, and the numbers on the right and the curvy line show temperature. You can see at a glance that St Louis is hottest in July, but December is the driest month.

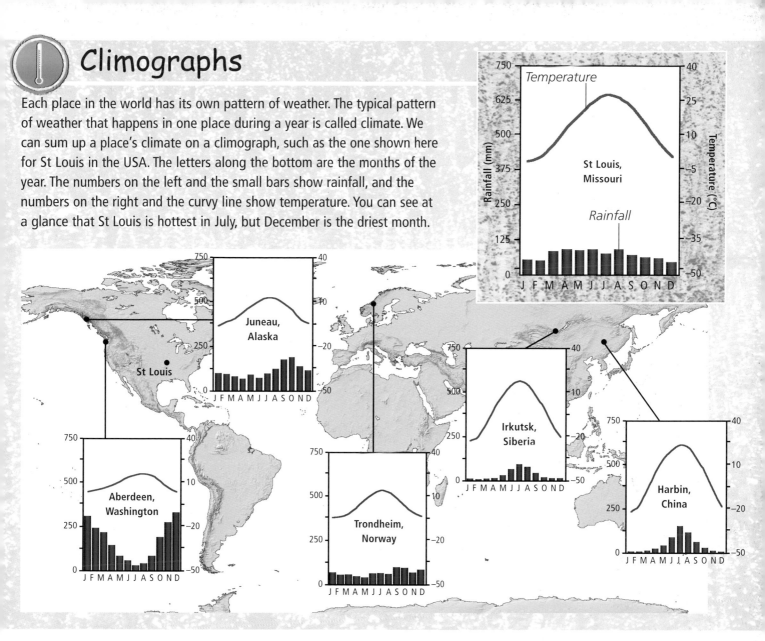

water dissolves metals such as iron and aluminium from the soil and deposits them deeper down. Sometimes, iron-rich layers called iron pans develop. Iron pans stop water from draining deeper into the ground. As a result, the soil above the iron pan becomes completely filled with water and this water drives all the air out of the soil.

In these conditions, plant material decomposes even more slowly. Over many hundreds of years, it accumulates to form **peat** – a brown mass of partially decayed vegetation. Dried peat can be burned as fuel. When peat is burned, the sunlight energy trapped by plants hundreds or thousands of years ago is released as heat.

History of soil

Scientists can unlock the ancient history of the taiga from its peat. **Pollen** grains – the microscopic capsules that contain the male sex cells of trees and other plants – are as recognizable as the flowers from which they come. But while flowers are fragile, pollen grains are armour-plated. They can survive preserved in peat for thousands of years.

The deeper the layer of peat, the older it is. Scientists collect the pollen grains from different layers and identify and count the grains under the microscope. This tells them which trees grew nearby thousands of years ago. It also tells them something about the climate at the time, and how this has

15

changed over the years. Changes in climate produce changes in plant life. The record of buried pollen charts the comings and goings of different plant species through time.

Permafrost

In parts of northern Canada and much of Siberia, the taiga grows above a solid layer of frozen ground. This permanently frosty soil is called **permafrost**. About 1 metre (3 ft) below the surface, the soil is rock-solid ice. Tree roots cannot penetrate this icy barrier and spread sideways to collect water.

The permafrost stops water from draining away, so the soil above becomes saturated with water. The trees themselves help create

Black spruce trees growing in open taiga in Labrador, Canada. The trees grow thickly in sheltered areas but are more scattered in exposed places.

the permafrost because they absorb the sun's heat, preventing it from reaching the icy ground. In parts of Siberia, the permafrost extends to more than 1250 metres (about 4000 ft) deep. Seeds buried in permafrost can be held in suspended animation for thousands of years. Most of the preserved seeds die, but just occasionally, a seed survives.

Open and closed taiga

At the northern edge of the taiga, the temperatures are almost too cold for trees to survive. Further to the north, the trees give way to open tundra, while to the south of this boundary, open taiga grows. Because of the cold, the trees growing in open taiga are generally small and lean and more widely spaced than the trees growing further south. In North America, open taiga is dominated

Moss grows in a boggy clearing in a Siberian forest. This area is free of trees because the ground is far too wet for them to grow.

by black spruce. Between the widely spaced trees, plenty of sunlight reaches the ground. Lichens, shrubs and small ground-level plants flourish in these clearings.

In the warmer southern areas of taiga, liquid water is available to plants for longer periods of the year. Because of this, the trees grow more densely, producing closed taiga forest. The tree cover is often so thick that only a little light reaches the forest floor. Shrubs and other small plants have limited opportunity to survive here, except where natural clearings are created by fires, fallen trees or areas of marshy ground.

From bogs to forests

Low-lying hollows and depressions in the forest collect water from surrounding areas, and the soil becomes so wet that trees cannot grow at all. In these boggy, airless conditions, the **bacteria** that normally breaks down dead material cannot thrive, so pine needles and other debris that accumulate in the hollow decay very slowly. This creates good conditions for mosses, such as sphagnum. Such mosses change the character of the soil. Over decades, the mosses die away and become sediments that gradually fill the hollows. Eventually, the hollows become dry enough for trees to grow there.

North-eastern American taiga

The eastern belt of taiga in North America sprawls across ancient mountains and wet lowlands. The region's landscape, including the immense Hudson Bay, was created by massive glaciers.

The beauty of this lake in Ontario is typical of the hundreds that are scattered through the region. Some of the lakes are popular holiday destinations.

 Fact file

▲ More than half of Canada's electricity comes from hydroelectric power stations in the taiga.

▲ Michigan is known as the Wolverine State. Trappers would bring wolverine furs and those of other taiga animals to trading posts in the state.

▲ Half of Canada's population is clustered in towns and cities around the St Lawrence River. Farmers have cleared most of the forests along the river.

1. Lake Superior
The world's largest surface area of fresh water. It covers almost the same area as Ireland.

2. Ouimet Canyon
A gorge 152 metres (500 ft) wide and 107 metres (350 ft) deep.

3. Hudson Bay
This massive bay is ice-locked from November to July.

4. Canadian Shield
A flat area that was once a towering range of mountains.

5. Adirondack Mountains
An area of taiga wilderness popular with hikers.

6. Charlevoix Reserve
A protected region of taiga, broad-leaved forests and wetlands. The area contains also the 700-metre (2200-ft) Hautes-Gorges, which are the deepest in eastern Canada.

7. Réservoir Manicouagan
A vast asteroid crater that has been made into the world's sixth-largest reservoir.

8. Acadia National Park
Reserve protecting America's most southerly taiga forest.

9. Labrador
A large peninsula in north-eastern Canada. Its rugged coast of fiords and islands was formed by glaciers.

10. Newfoundland
The main island in the larger province of the same name, visited by Viking explorers 500 years before Columbus's first voyage to America.

Hudson
Bay

• Churchill

NORTH
AMERICA
EUROPE
ASIA
AFRICA
SOUTH
AMERICA
AUSTRALIA
ANTARCTICA

N

Labrador Sea

9

CANADA

NEWFOUNDLAND

3

rshy lowlands

TOBA

James
Bay

4

7

Réservoir
Manicouagan

10

St John's

ONTARIO

QUEBEC

S h i e l d

C a n a d i a n

Lake Nipigon

Charlevoix
Reserve

Gulf of
St Lawrence

PRINCE
EDWARD I.

2

Ouimet
Canyon

6

St Lawrence River

NEW
BRUNSWICK

NOVA SCOTIA

• Halifax

1

Lake Superior

Quebec

MAINE

Atlantic Ocean

WISCONSIN

Lake Michigan

Lake Huron

Ottawa

• Montreal

5

Acadia
National Park

8

MICHIGAN

Toronto •

Lake Ontario

Adirondack
Mountains

Lake Erie

NEW YORK

• Boston

Chicago •

PENNSYLVANIA

0   250   miles

ILLINOIS

INDIANA

OHIO

U S A

0   250   500 km

Developing the wilderness

In the last 30 years, Canada's national and provincial governments have had to decide how to best protect the taiga wilderness while providing energy and raw materials for the country's expanding population. Between 1975 and 1990, the Cree and Inuit people around the southern part of Hudson Bay lost 15,500 square kilometres (6000 sq miles) of their land to dams (right) and generating stations to provide power for Quebec and Ontario. Since then, plans to further develop the wilderness have been subject to stricter controls.

Taiga plants

Trees dominate the taiga, but taiga forests do not have the lush diversity of tropical forests. Taiga plants have to live in extreme conditions, and only a few species are strong enough to survive.

About 2000 different species of conifer, flowering plants, ferns and mosses live in the world's taiga forests. This is far fewer than the number of species living in forests in warmer parts of the world. The majority of taiga trees belong to a mere dozen or so species, most of which are **evergreen** conifers with needle-like leaves.

Since the end of the last **ice age**, some 10,000 years ago, **glaciers** have slowly retreated from today's taiga regions. Glaciers still flow through some taiga forests, such as those in parts of Alaska and Norway. Because of the harsh conditions only a few species have evolved to survive there. The present taiga plants and animals only moved in once the ice had retreated.

Only a few hardy plants live in the taiga. Huge areas might be covered by a few species of trees.

The needles of a silver fir tree. These waxy spikes stay on the tree all year round and can withstand ice, snow and high winds.

Life in the cold

In many parts of the taiga, tree roots cannot penetrate very far into the soil before they reach the rock-solid permafrost. They have to get all their water and nutrients from the top 1 metre (3 ft) or so of soil. During the freezing winters, when liquid water is in very short supply, taiga plants need to hold onto all the water they can get.

The conifers' needle-like leaves have a thick, waxy coating that stops water from leaking out. The coating also acts like a suit of armour, giving the leaf strength. Like the leaves of most large plants, conifer needles absorb the gases they need and get rid of waste gases through tiny holes called stomata. Conifer stomata are often sunken into grooves, which avoids their losing too much water while taking in and giving out gases.

Dense taiga forests create their own cushioned environment. The sheltered, shaded conditions trap moist air, reduce wind speeds and keep temperature changes to a minimum. Most conifers are evergreen – they keep their leaves all year around. They can photosynthesize (trap sunlight to make food)

and grow whenever the sun is shining, although most growing occurs during the short, warm summers. The trees' needles are angled so they can collect sunlight coming from all directions.

Larches survive in the coldest conditions of all. Although they are conifers, they shed their leaves in winter to reduce water loss and frost damage. They have shallow, widespread roots that capture whatever water is available and also anchor the trees in the ground to withstand gales.

 # Fact file

▲ In 1915, a fire in Siberia burned an area roughly five times the size of Spain and Portugal.

▲ Trembling and quaking aspens get their name from the quivering effect of the leaves in the breeze.

▲ Many conifer trees are cone-shaped. Heavy snow slides off the downwards-sloping branches, so it does not weigh down and damage the tree.

21

Hidden partnership

Beneath the forest floor is a complex network of **fungi**, whose thread-like feeding tubes, or **hyphae**, permeate the soil. Hyphae are the underground parts of fungi. We notice the presence of fungi only when they produce mushrooms and toadstools above the surface.

Many fungal hyphae form partnerships with tree roots, entwining around them or even growing inside them. Such partnerships are called **mycorrhizae**. The hyphae in mycorrhizae digest dead matter in the soil, releasing nutrients for both themselves and the tree. Besides providing nutrients, mycorrhizae protect trees from disease and harmful soil bacteria, by producing

A rain-covered mushroom sits among spruce saplings. Fungi play a very important role in the life of taiga trees.

antibiotics (bacteria-killing substances). In return, trees create the right conditions for mycorrhizae to flourish. They shed dead needles for the fungi to feed on, and their roots provide a supply of sugar. All in all, the partnership works well for both. Without the mycorrhizae, conifer forests would not grow as thickly as they do. Smaller taiga plants, including wild flowers such as orchids, rely on mycorrhizae to survive on the forest floor.

Trees dominate

For a small plant, it is a tough life trying to grow on the floor of a thick conifer forest. The trees cut out the sunlight, they take water and nutrients from the soil and they

This pine drop plant is an unusual species that grows in North American taiga. Pine drops do not photosynthesize but get food by breaking down fallen pine needles.

shed twigs and needles that can smother a growing plant. Worse than that, the needles contain toxic substances that stop other plants from growing nearby. Few plants can thrive under a dense forest **canopy**. But if a clearing forms when a tree falls over or burns down, smaller plants have a chance to gain a foothold. They grow quickly and spread their seeds before a new tree takes over the space. Their seeds lie in the soil waiting for another clearing to open up.

Layer upon layer

A few shrubs, such as junipers, wild roses and alders, do grow below the conifer canopy. The shrubs' fruits provide food for forest animals, which may also shelter among the plants' tangled branches.

Lower down at ground level, cowberry, bilberry and twinflower plants grow in scattered patches, particularly where the tree cover is sparse. Where the soil is damp, lichens and mosses hug the ground. Higher up, other lichens grow on branches and tree trunks wherever the air is clean. Their absence is a sign that the air is polluted.

The plants of the forest floor grow in dim light. In fact, were they to be placed in bright sunlight most would shrivel and die. Some forest-floor plants bear nectar-rich flowers to attract insects to pollinate them. Generally, these plants – cowberries, wintergreens and starflowers, among them – have white flowers. These are bold signals to attract bees and butterflies in the forest gloom.

Nature's larder

The seeds and fruits of trees and shrubs are the main food source for many of the taiga's animals, including squirrels, chipmunks and birds such as nutcrackers and crossbills. Although this seems like bad news for the plants, they, too, can benefit. For example, nutcrackers and crossbills eat the seeds of Swiss stone pine. At least some of the seeds pass through the birds' digestive systems unharmed. When they land on the ground, the birds' droppings provide a helpful dollop of natural fertilizer. Brown bears and capercaillies perform a similar service in spreading juniper and bilberry seeds.

Animals also disperse seeds and fruits without having to eat them. The tiny, spiny fruit of the twinflower catches on the fur of small mammals and the feathers of birds. The animals may travel far and wide before the fruit drops to the ground.

In death, life
The thick layer of pine needles on the forest floor takes time to break down. Gradually, the poisons inside the needles are washed out by rain, and the needles become brittle and vulnerable to attack. Armies of small animals, such as springtail insects, soil mites, woodlice and earthworms, eat the needles and other buried debris. As the plant matter is broken down into smaller and smaller

What is a cone?

Most mature conifers produce scaly structures called cones. A cone is a conifer's equivalent to a flower. Male cones tend to be smaller and mature earlier than female cones. They produce pollen grains, which are released into the air when the cone's scales open up (right). The pollen is carried on the wind and caught in open female cones. The male and female sex cells fuse inside the female cone and produce seeds. The female cones then close up, and the scales do not open again until the seeds are ripe. The ripe seeds fall out of the cones and drop to the ground or travel on the wind, until they land in a suitable place to grow. The entire breeding process, from the growth of cones to the release of the seeds, takes about fifteen months.

chunks, fungi and bacteria finish off the decaying process that the animals began. The chemicals locked up in the dead plant material are gradually returned to the soil.

Do-it-yourself

Plants do not always rely on animals to transport pollen, or to scatter fruits and seeds. Many plants are able to produce seeds without having to receive pollen from another plant. For example, the common wood sorrel and May lily produce white flowers to attract insects, but they can pollinate themselves if necessary. They can also produce new plants by growing underground stems that establish independent roots and shoots nearby.

Mosses and lichens

Mosses carpet the tree trunks and ground in damp taiga. They photosynthesize, but unlike seed-producing plants such as trees and wild flowers, they have no true leaves. Mosses also take up water and nutrients from the soil, but they do not have proper roots. They can reproduce sexually, but they release

The silver fronds growing among this cowberry bush are lichens, confusingly named reindeer moss.

25

sperm into water, rather than producing pollen grains. The sperm swim to other plants and fertilize their female sex cells. Mosses are simple, miniature plants, but they have some major advantages over larger plants. They can withstand drying out. Some types can lose three-quarters of their water – becoming leathery tufts – but swell up and spring back to life again when water returns. And mosses can absorb water and dissolved minerals directly from snow and rain. They do not need to have roots in the soil.

Lichens are even hardier than mosses. They are a partnership between fungi and **algae** (simple plant-like organisms). The algae photosynthesize and provide food, while the fungi absorb water and minerals from the rain and snow. The fungi also form protective sheaths around the fragile algae. These sheaths shrink and close in dry conditions when water could be lost, and open again when moisture returns. Lichens thrive on moist bark and fallen wood. Beautifully sculpted lichens, such as the fine

Fire in the taiga

Fire in taiga forests sounds like bad news, but many of the trees can cope with heat and flames. Larches and pines have thick bark that offers good protection against fire damage. (Spruces and firs, however, tend to have thinner bark and shallow roots that are damaged by fire.) The cones of jack pines release their seeds only after a fire. The heat makes the cones explode, releasing the seeds, which then have a good

chance of germinating in the ash-covered clearing created by the fire. Flames and searing heat also sterilize the forest floor and kill off disease-causing organisms and parasites. Fires clear space for new trees to grow (below), and the ash adds nutrients to the soil. Following a fire, a rich variety of small ground plants grow, until the hardy coniferous trees and other taiga plants gradually take over once again.

strands of one species called old man's beard, cover branches. Some lichens growing on trees produce acids that have antibiotic properties. They may even protect their host trees from attacks by wood-destroying fungi.

Dark conifers

The dark conifers – the spruces and firs – are so-called because their leaves are very dark green. When seen from an aircraft, these trees darken large areas of forest. In European taiga, Norway spruce is the most common species. In Asia, the Siberian spruce is the dominant dark conifer.

Taiga plants of North America

The trees that grow in the North American taiga are typical of taiga around the world. Hardy larches survive in the far north. Spruces and firs cover the main parts of the region, while deciduous trees, such as birches, become more common further south. The coastal forests of giant redwood trees, however, are unique. No other taiga gets so much rain, and these forests are lusher than in other areas.

Larch trees live at the northern edge of taiga.

Black spruces grow in cold conditions.

Douglas firs are common in mountain forest.

Paper birches are deciduous trees that live in southern taiga.

Redwoods, the world's largest trees, grow in forests along the Pacific North-west coast.

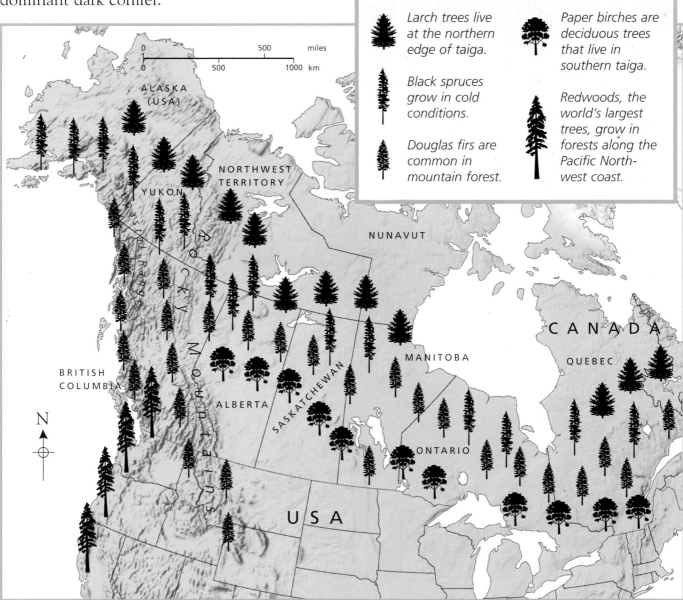

Mosses grow best in damp places. In the Hoh Rainforest in Washington State in the USA, mosses almost completely cover the trees, thanks to the high rainfall.

Spruces grow slowly and need damp soil all year around. In winter, these trees look particularly attractive because the pale snow contrasts heavily with their dark foliage. Spruce forests have a place in Nordic folklore, which says that they are home to mischievous gnomes, goblins and trolls.

In North America, the black (or bog) spruce is a common dark conifer. These trees are generally small and hardy and grow in very cold and boggy conditions. The white spruce is a taller dark conifer that grows in warmer, better-drained soil in the region.

Fir trees do not grow as far north as spruces. They require milder conditions and more fertile soils. The Douglas fir of North America is one of the world's largest trees, growing 100 metres (330 ft) tall, with a trunk 5 metres (16 ft) across. They form forests in the Rocky Mountains and grow in mixed forests close to the Pacific North-west coast.

 Christmas trees

In Europe and North America, people buy conifers to decorate their homes at Christmas. Different species are chosen in different countries, depending on availability and local preferences. In North America, for example, the Douglas fir is popular; in parts of Europe, Norway spruce is the favourite.

The link between conifers and Christmas goes back more than 1000 years. According to tradition, St Boniface, an English missionary in Germany in the 8th century AD, stumbled across people worshipping an oak tree dedicated to the god Thor. In anger, Boniface cut down the tree, and a fir tree began to grow in its place. Since then, fir trees have been linked with Christian worship.

Light conifers

Light conifers have paler leaves and include most pines and larches. They are more widely distributed than dark conifers because they can tolerate a broader range of conditions. The Scotch pine is the most common light conifer, covering much of the European and Asian taiga. In North America, jack pine

This patch of southern forest taiga has both evergreen and deciduous trees. The deciduous aspen trees have shed their leaves, while the conifers (rear) keep their needles.

takes the lead. Larches are light conifers that shed their leaves. They can resist extreme cold and grow further north than any other type of tree.

Deciduous trees

A few deciduous trees, which shed leaves in winter, grow in taiga. Birches, aspens and poplars grow in warmer, southern regions. European white birch and trembling aspen grow in Europe and Asia, and white birch and quaking aspen live in North America.

European taiga

The European taiga stretches right across the continent from Scotland to the Urals of Russia. In western Europe, taiga forests grow around lakes and wetlands. In the east, the forest covers a huge, featureless lowland.

 ## Fact file

▲ Russia is in both Europe and Asia and is the world's largest country.

▲ About three-quarters of Finland is covered in forest and woodland.

▲ The Swedes and Finns manage their forests so that timber is not cut down faster than it is replaced.

▲ Rock outcrops across northern Scandinavia are 2.5 billion years old.

Background: An open forest in Lapland in northern Sweden. Lapland is home to the Sami people and spreads across the whole of northern Scandinavia.

0   400   miles
0   400   800 km

N

4
Stabbursdalen

Lapland

2

SWEDEN

Gulf of Bothnia

5

FINLAND

Pyhä-Hä

Stockholm

Helsinki

Oslo

Gulf of Finland

Atlantic Ocean

ESTONIA

NORWAY

LATVIA

1

North Sea

DENMARK

Baltic Sea

LITHUANIA

Edinburgh

Copenhagen

Kaliningrad

Minsk

IRELAND

UNITED KINGDOM

NETH.

Berlin

3

BELAR

BELG.

GERMANY

Warsaw

POLAND

Moving with the climate

People were living in northern taiga forests 100,000 years ago. But when the last ice age began about 70,000 years ago, the world cooled and glaciers spread as far south as Italy. The ice sheet forced the taiga south as well, and animals that were adapted to live in cold conditions, such as woolly mammoths (right), lived in regions that are now noted for their warm weather. The people of the taiga also moved south as the forests shifted. The ice has since retreated north, and taiga grows in its current location.

1. Scotland
Scottish taiga is scattered in small patches. Tree-felling, followed by sheep- and deer-grazing, have removed most of the original forest.

2. Sweden
Until the 1990s, Swedish conifers were badly affected by acid rain created by pollution from the UK and Germany.

3. Kaliningrad
This ancient seaport on the Baltic Sea is now part of an isolated Russian enclave.

4. Stabbursdalen
The Gulf Stream warms the climate of this Norwegian national park. Taiga forest grows further north here than anywhere else on Earth.

5. Pyhä-Häkki
A protected area of forest and peatland. Most trees here are more than 250 years old, and a few date from the 14th century.

6. St Petersburg, Russia
Called Leningrad during the communist era, this is Russia's largest seaport.

7. Karelia
This region has the most diverse taiga forests and wetlands in Europe.

8. Lake Ladoga
At 18,100 square km (7000 sq miles), this is the largest lake in Europe and has a maximum depth of 225 metres (738 ft).

9. Kola Peninsula
This part of Scandinavia is in Russia. It is an important mining centre and has several hydroelectric plants along its fast-flowing rivers.

10. Volga River
The Volga, flowing 3530 km (2193 miles), is the longest river in Europe. It empties into the Caspian Sea in Russia.

11. Pechoro-Ilychskiy Nature Reserve
This large reserve – at 6880 square km (2656 sq miles) – is mostly covered in taiga forest.

12. Ural Mountains
The Ural Mountains separate Europe from Asia. The region is rich in metals such as copper, nickel, gold and platinum.

Taiga animals

Despite the long months of snow and ice, a wide variety of animals eke out an existence in taiga forests, including some of the largest land animals in the world. Most live alone among the forest trees, rarely crossing each other's path.

The long, hard winter of the taiga presents a great challenge for most animals living there. Thick snow makes it difficult for larger animals to move about, and the snow covers food on the ground.

Most of the large animals of the taiga feed on plant material, such as leaves, fruit and seeds. In the long winter, deer have to exist on tree bark, mosses and lichens. Chipmunks, woodmice and squirrels rely on hidden stores of seeds and summer fruits.

As for the smallest creatures, such as insects and other invertebrates, many live underneath tree bark, among the leaf litter and buried in the soil. In the cold season, they hide away in a **dormant** (inactive) state or they overwinter as eggs or young. Some of these animals have natural antifreeze in their

In summer, taiga forests are filled with biting insects. The insects spend the winter as dormant pupae and develop into adults as the warm weather begins.

Canadian moose are at home in shallow water (right), where they feed on soft aquatic plants. In winter these large deer eat less, surviving mainly on bark.

body fluids. This substance stops them from freezing to death. Most taiga invertebrates feed on detritus – the dead remains of plants and animals. Others feed on the heartwood of trees, deep inside their trunks.

Because the taiga is so cold, and conifer needles contain many waxy and toxic substances, dead plant matter takes a long time to break down. In summer, an army of slugs, millipedes, woodlice and beetles feeds on the decomposing plant matter. As they break it down, they release nutrients and return them to the soil.

Eaten alive

At the height of the short summer, taiga forests are filled with flying insects, many of which bite larger animals. The air is alive with millions of mosquitoes and blackflies feasting on the blood of **mammals** – including

Wolves spend the winter living in packs. They hunt as a team, travelling large distances in pursuit of prey. In summer the packs disband and wolves may hunt alone.

people. Only the female flies feed on blood – to provide enough energy to produce their eggs. The males eat flower nectar and plant sap. Mosquitoes lay their eggs in water, where their larvae hatch and grow. If the summer is particularly dry, there will be far fewer mosquitoes than usual. A warm, wet summer, however, is good for mosquitoes.

Deer

Elk and reindeer are the taiga's largest plant eaters. Reindeer, which are called caribou in North America, migrate from tundra to taiga in winter, but elk – called moose in North America, where another deer is called the elk – tend to remain in the taiga all year round.

The elk is lord of the taiga and the world's largest species of deer. Males are more than 1.8 metres (6 ft) tall at the shoulder and can weigh 500 kg (1100 lbs). Despite their large size, elk are shy and peaceful animals. With keen senses of smell and hearing, they generally disappear into the forest when disturbed. Nevertheless, if confronted, an elk can defend itself well. Using antlers reaching up to 2 metres (79 in) across, and kicking with its sharp hooves, a healthy adult male can fend off all but the worst wolf attacks. However, the males use their antlers more often in ritual fights with rivals over access to female mates.

Elk prefer to graze on the leaves and fruit of small plants at the edges of the forest and in clearings. They have a large appetite and can eat around 15 kg (33 lbs) of food a day in winter and an incredible 35 kg (77 lbs) daily in summer.

These deer spend long periods close to ponds and rivers, because there are plenty of edible plants in the water and along the banks. In summer, they sometimes submerge themselves for hours on end to avoid the swarms of biting insects. The water is also a haven from marauding wolves. In winter,

with food very scarce, elk eat strips of tree bark. A large population of elk can devastate forests this way.

Wood bison live in the southern parts of the North American taiga. These very rare animals are not deer but are closely related to other cattle-like bison that once lived in the open prairies to the south.

Pack hunters

Unlike all other taiga **predators**, grey wolves hunt co-operatively. In deep winter, when food is scarce, they gather together to track down and overpower even the largest deer. In summer, they are more likely to hunt separately, going after much smaller prey, such as squirrels and marmots.

 # A pale shadow

Thick fur or feathers keep many taiga animals warm in winter. Some of the taiga's mammals – the snow-shoe hare and the stoat, for instance – turn white in winter. This change of colour serves as camouflage in a snow-covered landscape, allowing the hare (below) to hide from predators more easily, and the stoat to sneak up on its victims. Pale fur may offer better insulation than dark fur. Some scientists believe that dark pigment (coloured chemical) thickens the hair. Pale fur is thinner, leaving more space between the hairs to trap warm air, and this improves insulation.

The female capercaillie is smaller and less conspicuous than the male. The males use their distinctive plumage in complex displays to attract mates.

The wolf pack – a family group of eight to twelve wolves led by a single male and female pair – tracks its quarry by smell. Wolves can smell their prey from almost 2 km (over 1 mile) away. Once they pick up a scent, they cluster together – like American football players in a huddle – before setting off in pursuit. What messages they pass to one another at this time – by growls, a flick of the ear, a shake of the head – are still a mystery.

Once the wolves get close to their prey, they begin the attack. The onslaught is triggered by the victim fleeing in fright. The wolves take turns jumping onto the head, rump, back or flanks of the prey, inflicting bites that injure and gradually weaken it. Little by little, the panic-stricken animal is overpowered and then torn to pieces. Each wolf gobbles down as much meat as it can manage. Adult wolves can gorge 9 kg (20 lbs) at a single sitting.

Despite their reputation and bloodthirsty hunting techniques, wolves are really timid creatures. There are few, if any, properly documented examples of wolves attacking and killing people. In fact, people are a much

 ## When big is best

In a cold environment, large size can be an advantage. Larger creatures have smaller body surface areas compared to their weights than smaller creatures, helping large animals conserve heat better. This is why male stoats from northern Canada weigh about three times as much as their cousins in milder forests in the USA. It also helps explain why many taiga animals are record breakers: the elk is the world's largest deer, the wolverine the largest weasel and bears (right) are the largest land predators.

and on the ground. Many birds nest in taiga forest trees, raise their young and then fly south to spend the winter in warmer areas.

Taiga fighter

Few birds remain in the taiga all year round. Among those that do are woodpeckers, crossbills, nuthatches and, biggest of all, the capercaillie. This bulky bird, a type of grouse weighing up to 6 kg (13 lbs), feeds on wild fruits in summer and autumn and resorts to a diet of pine needles in winter. In the cold season, capercaillies stay in trees during the

bigger danger to wolves than the other way around. Hunters shooting wolves over the last 200 years have massively reduced wolf numbers around the world.

Summer visitors

The arrival of spring in the taiga fills the air with birdsong. Many of the taiga's birds, such as Siberian rubythroats, are summer visitors. They fly north to take advantage of the abundant insect life on the trees, in the air

A black woodpecker mother feeds two hungry chicks. This large species of woodpecker lives right across Europe and Asia, including northern Japan.

day and bury themselves in snow to pass the night. In the summer, a male capercaillie stridently defends his territory against other males. When a resident male spots another male approaching, he gives a call that sounds a little like a cork being pulled from a bottle. If the call has no effect, the defending male drops to the ground and prepares to fight the invader. The fight begins as a ritual in which the birds pretend to bite each other. If one does not back down, the confrontation can degenerate into a brawl, with one bird clasping the neck of the other. If the males are well matched, they fight until one is seriously injured or dead. The winner controls the territory and has access to females.

Head-bangers

The black woodpecker is the largest and loudest woodpecker in Europe and Asia. It uses its chisel-like beak to excavate holes in tree trunks and pry off bark to reveal hidden

A Clark's nutcracker perches on top of a conifer tree. This species lives in the conifer forests of the Rocky Mountains, where it feeds on seeds and insects.

Hunting in the snow

In winter, much of the taiga is covered in snow around 1 metre (3 ft) deep, and temperatures plunge to −40°C (−40°F). The small forest predators hunt beneath the snow. There, weasels and stoats pursue shrews and rodents, such as squirrels. Shrews, in turn, hunt insects, while the rodents search for pine cones.

Large animals have difficulty moving through the deep snow. The exceptions are wolverines, which have broad feet that act like snowshoes. The wolverine's dense, long fur is another aid in icy weather. It does not freeze, even when wet.

The wolverine (below) − known also as a glutton in Europe and Asia − belongs to the weasel family. It has a remarkable reputation for strength and aggressiveness, out of all proportion to its size. Although it grows to only 27 kg (60 lbs) in weight, a wolverine can take on a reindeer or an elk floundering in deep snow. Sometimes a wolverine stumbles through a camper's tent, wrecking the contents along the way.

Wolverines are solitary animals, except during the brief breeding season. They eat small rodents, eggs, young birds and insects, supplemented with wild fruits and pine seeds. They also eat carrion, sometimes following wolf packs to scavenge for scraps left behind. Wolverines have even been known to drive bears from their kills.

People rarely see wolverines because they are so secretive. Females give birth to two or three cubs in mid to late winter, safe within a den under snow and often beneath a fallen tree. The young can hunt for themselves by the end of their first summer.

European taiga animals

Fewer large animals live in taiga than in other biomes. Many of these animals spend long periods without seeing another member of their own species. Despite being small in number, these species are spread over a wide area. Many, such as wolves and bears, live in all parts of the biome and also reside south of the taiga belt. Elk and bears spend the summer in barren tundra to the north of the taiga.

 Elk. Most common in Scandinavia.

 Grey wolf. Lives in packs in most parts of taiga.

 Black woodpecker. The largest woodpecker in the region.

 Reindeer. Spends winter in taiga.

 Brown bear. A large, solitary omnivore.

 Wolverine. A large, weasel-like predator.

insects. It is not unusual for these voracious birds to eat a thousand ants or beetle larvae (young) during a single meal.

The holes these woodpeckers make provide homes for other creatures, from owls to red squirrels and, by breaking up rotten wood, the birds speed up the recycling of nutrients. The black woodpecker has a remarkable tongue that extends over 5 cm (2 in) beyond its bill. It is pointed and covered in hook-like barbs that stick into food.

Like other woodpeckers, these birds' brains are cushioned by a sac of fluid enclosed within a thick skull. These structures absorb the thousands of blows delivered by the bird's bill each day. The sound of a woodpecker's drilling can be heard over a kilometre away.

Nutcrackers and crossbills

Some birds are highly dependent on the seeds of conifer trees. Nutcrackers use their powerful beaks to crush and batter pine and spruce cones, releasing the seeds. Crossbills are more delicate – they pry open the cones to extract the seeds. Different species of crossbill have beaks suited to particular types of cone. In Siberia, the parrot crossbill uses a robust, rounded beak to extract seeds from tough pine cones, while the two-barred crossbill, with a much thinner bill, goes for the more delicate cones of the larch.

Crossbills are the only taiga birds that breed during winter. They can extract seeds from cones throughout the winter, providing a year-round supply of food. Nutcrackers breed in spring. In autumn, they bury supplies of seeds under the snow to see them through the hard times ahead.

Voles

Forest voles are tiny rodents, with adults weighing only about 40 g (1.5 oz). They avoid the worst of the winter by digging tunnels in snow; the air-filled snow is a good insulator against the cold weather outside. Under the snow, voles search for buried nuts and soft fruits. In summer, their diet is much more varied, including seeds, leaves, mushrooms, soft fruits, lichens, bark and insects. Like most rodents, they can breed quickly when conditions are favourable, producing up to five litters a year.

Squirrels

Squirrels and chipmunks eat pine nuts and bury cones in a winter food store. Red squirrels use their sharp incisor teeth to gnaw the scales off spruce and pine cones to get at the seeds. They are active almost all year round and keep moving during summer, searching for fresh cones. In winter, they rely on food they have buried. A red squirrel may bury 200 cones in a day. Uneaten seeds begin growing into trees the following spring.

Crossbills are so called because the tips of their bills cross over like a pair of scissors. This helps them snip into cones to get at the seeds inside.

Miniature carnivores

Stoats and weasels are the small predators of the taiga – long, sleek and agile, they are rarely more than 24 cm (9 in) from head to tail and weigh less than 200 g (7 oz). The stoat – with its pale, thick winter coat – was a favourite quarry of trappers. The pale winter fur, called ermine, was used for making ceremonial robes. In 1937, Canada exported 50,000 ermine pelts to the UK for the coronation of King George VI. Some 300 pelts were needed to make a single gown.

Stoats mate during the summer, but the babies do not develop inside the females' womb until many months later. This delays

A hoary marmot keeps a lookout for danger in an Alaskan forest clearing. These large rodents give a range of alarm calls when they spot predators.

pregnancy and so ensures that young are born the following spring, after the thaw, when food is easier to find.

Silent but deadly

The great grey owl of the Russian taiga looks much larger than its true body size because of its thick downy feathers. These are good for keeping out the cold, but they also dampen any sounds during flight. The owl hunts by listening for the delicate scratchings of its

Bear feast

Fast, cold rivers flow through the taiga of Europe and North America. In some of these rivers, once a year a miraculous fishing event takes place. Salmon, fresh from the sea where they have been fattening themselves for several years, fight their way upriver to spawn (lay eggs). They battle to overcome all obstacles in their path – including waterfalls and fishing nets – in their desire to reach the spawning grounds. Salmon return to the very same stretches of river where they themselves hatched from eggs many years before. Predators, especially bears, relish this annual bonanza.

In the taiga forests of Canada and Russia, brown bears wait in the shallows at the base of rapids (below left). Here, salmon gather before their fight upstream. The fish sometimes pack so densely that the bears just have to scoop their paws through the water to catch one.

For the chinook salmon of Alaska and northern Canada, spawning ends in the exhausted adults' death. Their decaying bodies fertilize the river water, encouraging plankton and plants to grow, and in turn small freshwater animals, such as insect larvae. The newly hatched salmon feed on these creatures.

prey – generally voles. Once located, the owl hovers above and then drops onto its prey, which may be deep below the snow. The owl plunges through the snow, seizes the victim in its talons and kills it with a bite to the back of the neck.

Coping with winter

Many taiga animals spend the cold winter inside warm nests in an inactive state. They eat as much as they can during the short summer and put on fat reserves to last them through winter. Nevertheless, many rely on food stores during the cold season. The Siberian chipmunk, for example, often leaves its nest to feast on its seed store.

Only a few taiga animals, such as the squirrel-like marmot, **hibernate**. They become dormant for long periods, their pulse and breathing rates drop to a fraction of their normal level and they do not feed. Even so, they wake every few weeks to get rid of urine, and they stir during the coldest spells to avoid freezing to death. Contrary to popular belief, bears are not true hibernators. They do not sleep right through the winter, but wake up at intervals. A mother brown bear, for example, wakes regularly to suckle her cubs.

Siberian taiga

The Siberian taiga is the world's largest forest – it covers an area twice that of the Amazon rainforest. It is crossed by some of the world's biggest rivers, down which timber companies float felled logs to sawmills and factories.

A village in western Siberia. Millions of Russians have moved into the taiga in the last 300 years.

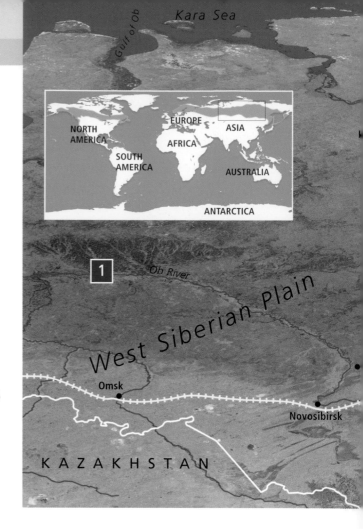

Kara Sea

Gulf of Ob

NORTH AMERICA

EUROPE

ASIA

AFRICA

SOUTH AMERICA

AUSTRALIA

ANTARCTICA

1

Ob River

West Siberian Plain

Omsk

Novosibirsk

KAZAKHSTAN

Siberia facts

▲ The Ural Mountains stop rain clouds from reaching western Siberia. To the east of the mountains the climate tends to be dry with bitterly cold winters and hot summers.

▲ The Trans-Siberian Railway crosses seven different time zones.

▲ The Siberian taiga is bordered by the Arctic tundra in the north and the Kazakh and Mongolian steppes (grasslands) in the south.

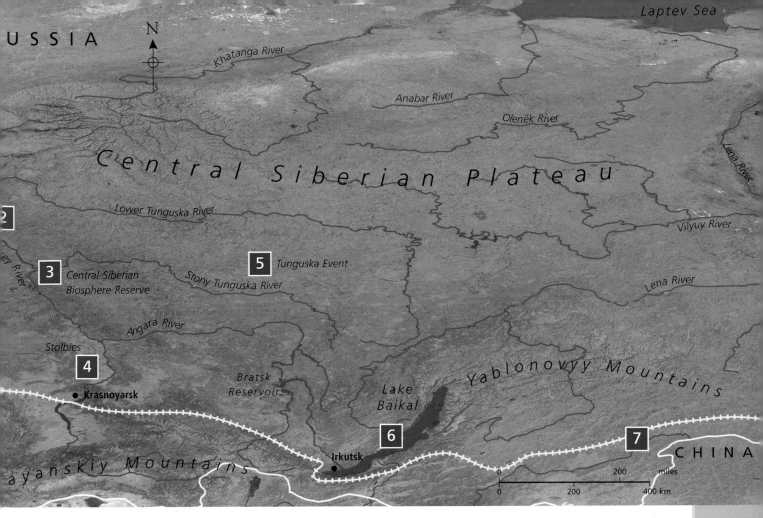

RUSSIA

Laptev Sea

Khatanga River

Anabar River

Olenëk River

Lena River

C e n t r a l   S i b e r i a n   P l a t e a u

Lower Tunguska River

Vilyuy River

2

3 *Central Siberian Biosphere Reserve*

...ey River

5 *Tunguska Event*

Stony Tunguska River

Lena River

Angara River

Stolbies

4

Bratsk Reservoir

Lake Baikal

Yablonovyy Mountains

● **Krasnoyarsk**

6

7

...ayanskiy Mountains

Irkutsk ●

CHINA

0 — 200 — miles
0 — 200 — 400 km

1. Ob River
At 5410 km (3362 miles) long, the Ob is Russia's longest river. It flows from the Altai Mountains close to the Mongolian border to the Gulf of Ob in the Arctic.

2. Yenisey River
This river is an important Siberian transport route. Timber is shipped around the world from Igarka. Some believe North America's earliest peoples came from this region.

3. Central Siberian Biosphere Reserve
A large taiga reserve in the homeland of the Evenki people, who carry on their traditional way of life.

4. Stolbies
Unique volcanic-rock formations created by wind and rain. Many stolbies are contained in a taiga nature reserve beside the Yenisey River. The tallest reaches 120 metres (366 ft) high.

5. Tunguska Event
On 30 June 1908, a huge meteorite smashed into the ground near the Stony Tunguska River. More than 2150 sq km (830 sq miles) of forest was destroyed, and, hundreds of miles away, trains were derailed by the impact.

6. Lake Baikal
Lake Baikal covers one and a half times the area of Wales. The lake holds the largest volume of fresh water of any lake in the world. In places, it is almost 2 km (over a mile) deep. More like a sea than a lake, it harbours 1500 unique plants and animals, including freshwater seals.

7. Trans-Siberian Railway
The world's longest railway. Along its 9299-km (5778-mile) route, from Moscow to Vladivostok, it crosses desert, mountain and forest. Express trains take seven days to travel the entire length.

Hidden wealth

7

Much of Russia's wealth lies beneath the taiga of Siberia. Most of Russia's petroleum oil and gas is drilled in western Siberia, while eastern Siberia sits upon huge coal deposits. Siberia's wood and coal are transported long distances to reach industrial centres in European Russia. Most of Siberia's rivers run into the Arctic Ocean and are often blocked by ice. The Trans-Siberian Railway (right), completed in 1904, is the main transport link for Siberia's produce.

People and the taiga

With little land suitable for agriculture or industry, the taiga has largely escaped the ravages of the modern world. In the past, people survived mainly by hunting, fishing and herding reindeer.

Compared to other land biomes, the human invasion of the taiga was slow, because the forests are so dense and the weather so extreme. The first people to live in taiga arrived by boat, travelling along major rivers, such as the Lena, Ob and Yenisey in Siberia, and the Mackenzie and Yukon in North America.

Archaeological evidence shows that people have lived in the taiga forests of Asia and Europe for more than 100,000 years. During ice ages throughout this period, ice sheets shifted south as the world cooled. The ice covered the land where taiga forests currently grow, and the biome was positioned further south than it is now. Each time the world warmed up again, the forests shifted north as the ice sheets melted away.

Over many thousands of years, people moved north and south with the gradual shifts of the taiga, and they were joined by new peoples, who migrated into the area from other biomes.

Above: A Khanty mother and child leave their tent in a summer camp in the taiga of European Russia. The Khanty spend the summer on the move with their herds.

People of the European and Asian taiga and tundra may well have been the first to colonize the Americas around 30,000 years ago, when people crossed a strip of land that once existed between Siberia and Alaska. Called the Bering Bridge, this land has since disappeared under the sea.

Siberian hunters

Around 2000 years ago, many of the peoples of the Siberian taiga, who had survived by hunting, began to raise herds of reindeer. They led a **nomadic** lifestyle, riding the reindeer or using them for carrying loads. The Evenki people of eastern Siberia would even hunt on deerback.

Nomadic people move from place to place in search of food and water. They must carry their homes with them, or hastily construct shelters from natural materials when they arrive at a new campsite. The Khanty people of northern Russia, for example, dig caves in the snow and cover the entrance with animal skins. In summer, some people make temporary tent-like shelters from poles covered in animal skin or birch bark.

Fishing people

Some European and Asian taiga peoples, including the Khanty, depended more on fishing than hunting. They led a more settled way of life than hunting people. In winter, they often came together in settlements of 150–170 people. They stored food at the settlement and went on short hunting expeditions in small family groups. When summer arrived, the families would leave for their fishing sites. Typically, one site supported two or three families.

Native Americans

Much less is known about the history of Native American taiga peoples before European settlers arrived. However, some early American history has been passed on in artwork, fables and folklore.

Below: A herd of reindeer is driven through taiga forest in Siberia. These deer are used by many taiga peoples for food, transport and clothing.

The members of a family of Alaskan Athabascans display the furs skinned from the animals they have trapped over the long taiga winter.

People probably began to colonize the present North American taiga about 12,000 years ago, as the Earth warmed after the last ice age. These people were ancestors of the **Algonquians** and **Athabascans** – two major groups originally from Asia, with different languages. Algonquians live in much of the eastern part of North America. The taiga-dwelling Algonquians live in the area of the Great Lakes, Hudson Bay and eastern Canada. The Athabascans live in Alaska, along the Pacific coast of North America and in the Rocky Mountains.

Both groups were hunters and fishers. Men hunted caribou (reindeer) and moose (which are called elk in Europe) and fished the rivers and lakes. Women and men

A totem pole, topped by an eagle sculpture, stands in the steep mountainous taiga forests of British Columbia.

Nothing wasted

The Nenet people of northern Siberia are reindeer herders. They live in wood-framed, conical tents covered with reindeer skin. Each family looks after a herd of about 70–100 reindeer, and when a deer is slaughtered, almost nothing is wasted. The Nenet eat deer meat, drink the deer's blood and use deer fat for cooking, fuel and waterproofing. The skin is made into clothes and shoes. The Nenet use deer tendons and sinews as sewing threads, and they carve antlers into attractive decorations or make them into tools.

gathered wild fruits, nuts and roots to supplement their diet of meat. In summer, communities tended to settle near lakes and rivers. In winter, they lived on the move, following the migrating caribou.

Totems

According to the spiritual traditions of many taiga peoples, several forest animals were sacred. Each clan believed it was descended from a particular type of animal, and these animals became revered emblems, or totems. Clan members believed it was wrong to hunt these sacred animals.

Among many Athabascan tribes, the wolf was a totem. It was forbidden to kill wolves, even if they had been attacking caribou herds. They believed that if a wolf was killed, the spirit world would take revenge and send more and more wolves to attack the herds.

The residents of taiga towns live close to nature. This moose is paying a visit to a home in Anchorage, Alaska.

Tribes on the Canadian west coast made totem poles – ornately carved wooden poles ranging from 2 metres (6 ft) to 16 metres (50 ft) tall. The poles served different functions: to ward off evil spirits, to honour certain animals or to record a clan's history.

The modern Russian taiga

Russians began migrating into the taiga forests east of the Ural Mountains in the 16th century. People cleared the forest around small settlements to make way for farms. Peasants from eastern Europe settled across the region to escape hardship and poverty in their own countries, and they lived fairly peacefully alongside the native taiga peoples. Siberia became a favoured place for Russian governments to send political rebels and criminals. Joseph Stalin, the tyrannical Russian leader, created an enormous network of prison camps there.

Today, most people living in the Siberian taiga are Russians or Ukrainians, rather than historical taiga peoples. They live in cities, such as Irkutsk, Tomsk and Yakutsk.

Taiga medicine

Across the taiga of North America, Europe and Asia, people use more than a thousand species of plants for medicines. Many fruits – among them gooseberries, cowberries and the fruits of magnolia – contain chemicals that have a stimulant effect. The fruits are consumed for several reasons, including improved blood flow and to stave off fatigue and hunger.

Traditionally, taiga peoples used extracts from a wide range of conifers to treat wounds and skin rashes. The Tanaina of north-west Canada make a tea from juniper branches to treat colds and pneumonia. Sphagnum moss from peat bogs has both antiseptic and absorbent properties. Native North Americans even used it to make nappies.

In Russia, chemicals from ginseng roots (right) were taken to produce a feeling of well-being. Ginseng is now a popular complementary medicine across Europe, America and China.

North American taiga today

Europeans began to colonize North America's taiga in the 17th century, with British people settling in the Hudson Bay region, and the French in Labrador and the St Lawrence River valley. In 1867, the USA purchased Alaska, originally colonized by Russia, for just $7.2 million – roughly £55 million in today's terms. A rich mix of people from Europe and Asia, as well as native descendants, live in Alaska today.

Most early colonizers began trading with Native American peoples of the taiga, but then, to a greater or lesser extent, exploited them and forced them to change their way of life. Today, about 30,000 people of Athabascan descent live in the taiga of Alaska, and north-west and central Canada. They include Tanaina, Tana and Chippewa tribes. To the east, among the 100,000 people of Algonquian descent that live in taiga regions, most belong to the Cree, who are historically hunters of caribou and moose. In European colonial days, the Cree traded with both British and French immigrants.

A few residents of the taiga, particularly those in more remote areas, still live a partly nomadic hunting and fishing lifestyle. Others are found on reservations and carry on a traditional way of life, living in tents. However, most native people have abandoned their previous lifestyles and adopted modern urban lives. They still retain their ethnic identity through clothing and art, by practicing traditional crafts and by taking part in dances and religious ceremonies.

A hard life

Living in the taiga has never been easy. Native peoples of the taiga were tough: the women gave birth by the campfire in freezing conditions while on the move from one hunting area to another. The newborn child was rubbed in snow before being held to the mother's breast. Even today, many taiga peoples live without benefit of local medical facilities. In the Siberian taiga, for example, the death rate among young babies is twice that of the Russian average.

Since the 1600s, greater contact with outsiders brought new diseases, such as smallpox, measles, influenza and tuberculosis, to which taiga peoples had little or no immunity. Colonizers also introduced alcohol. Many taiga peoples – for whom alcoholic drinks have never been a part of their culture – lack the enzyme that breaks down alcohol within the body. For them, drinking alcohol has a far greater intoxicating effect.

A young Mansi man rides through a river in the Ural Mountains of central Russia. Taiga peoples are finding it harder to maintain their way of life.

New diseases, exploitation by outsiders and the introduction of alcohol and drugs are among the many challenges taiga peoples have had to face. Nevertheless, in many native communities there is renewed awareness of the need to protect traditional values, customs and ways of life.

Modern hunting

The taiga's original peoples hunted animals in a sustainable way, so that local populations were not depleted. Since the 16th century, things have changed dramatically.

In the late 1500s, Russians began to colonize the Siberian taiga. The rising demand for fur sent hunters and trappers into the taiga in search of the valuable furs of foxes, beavers, minks and sables. Rivalry between the French and British over fur-rich territory in eastern Canada led to several wars in the region, with Native Americans fighting on both sides.

Fact file

▲ In the past, a Siberian hunter would kill up to 150 reindeer a year to feed and clothe his family.

▲ 13 square km (5 sq miles) of taiga forest produces enough food for just a single person.

▲ In the 1990s, the paper for 30 per cent of the world's newspapers came from Canadian forests.

▲ Today, most of Canada's furs come from fur farms.

By the 19th century, decades of hunting and trapping had massively reduced the populations of fur-bearing animals in the central and eastern parts of the North American taiga. Then, in the 1840s, the European demand for fur products dropped, as fur clothes became less fashionable. In the late 19th century, the Canadian government bought the land owned by the Hudson Bay Company and began controlling fur hunting.

Modern hunting methods – using high-power rifles and snowmobiles – are so efficient that, even in hostile terrain, local populations of rare fur animals can be wiped out quickly. Today, in many parts of taiga, there are bans on hunting sables, beavers, elk and some other types of deer.

Logging

Clear-felling – cutting down all the trees in an area of forest – began hundreds of years ago in the taiga of Scandinavia and Russia to supply wood for building ships. From the 1600s onwards, loggers in parts of Sweden and Finland also felled trees to provide fuel for the iron industry. Now, little of the original forest remains. However, by the late 1800s, the Scandinavians found that felled conifer forest could re-grow, given the chance. This was a better option than turning the land over to farming. The Canadians learned from the Scandinavian experience, and by the late 1870s, they began replanting some of their felled conifer forests.

Clear-felling can cause problems. In the Russian taiga, some felled areas have turned into bog. On slopes, clear-felling can lead to

A clear-felled stretch of taiga cuts through the mature forest. Conifer trees quickly re-populate clear-felled areas, but environmental damage still occurs.

Birch-bark canoes

Native Americans of the Canadian north-east used the bark of the white birch to make canoes (left). They stretched sheets of bark over a cedar frame, sewing them into place with the pliable roots of white spruce. Holes were sewn up and waterproofed with pine resins. The canoes were very light, with a flat bottom, and hunters could easily carry them around obstacles in a river, as they hunted for caribou or moose.

soil **erosion**, causing nearby rivers to fill with silt. Logjams add to the problem, blocking rivers. This has happened in some parts of European Russia and Siberia. Meanwhile, any remaining soil cover may be washed away, making it difficult for trees to re-establish themselves, as well as making the land unsuitable for agriculture. Today, loggers are encouraged to fell trees with more care, thinning the forest by selectively removing only some of the trees.

Mining

Over the centuries, people have been drawn to the Canadian and Russian taiga in search of gold and other precious metals. Many of the mines and smelters (metal extraction plants) have grown without adequate environmental controls. Mines create craters and heaps of unwanted dirt and rock. They are serviced by roads and temporary settlements that cut into the forest. Smelters produce pollution, which is spread around the taiga by the wind and rivers.

Fossil fuels

In the 1960s, huge reserves of oil and natural gas were discovered in Siberia. This made Russia one of the world's largest fuel producers and created great wealth – but at the expense of the environment. In the taiga's harsh climate, the pipelines and drilling facilities are not easy to maintain, and leaks are common. During the 1990s, there were several oil pollution incidents every year in Siberia. In western Canada, pipelines carrying fuels south from Alaska spring leaks that also damage the forest.

Miners pan and dig for gold in the Klondike Mountains of north-western Canada during the gold rush at the beginning of the 20th century.

Taiga

East Asian taiga

The East Asian taiga is home to some of the world's rarest animals, including Siberian tigers and snow leopards. Because of the region's wet summers and cool winters, the taiga extends further south here than elsewhere in Asia.

Steam escapes from volcanic vents in a mountain in Kamchatka. Thousands of years of volcanic activity in this region have produced very fertile soils.

 ## Fact file

▲ Large-scale deforestation and acid rain have damaged much of Japan's taiga forest.

▲ Houses in Yakutsk are built on stilts to keep the buildings' heat from melting the permafrost beneath.

▲ Siberian tigers are the world's largest cats. In winter their red-striped fur becomes paler so they do not stand out against the snow.

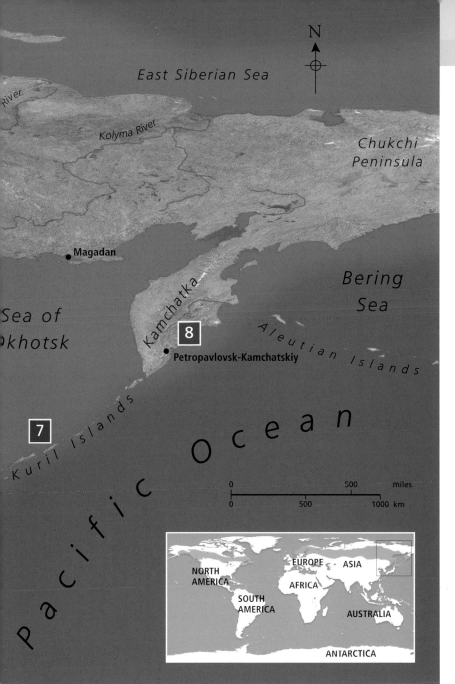

East Asian taiga

1. Lena River
One of the longest rivers in the world, flowing 4400 km (2734 miles) from its source in the mountains west of Lake Baikal to the Arctic.

2. Heilongjiang
Although it is close to one of the most heavily industrialized regions of China, Heilongjiang province is still thickly forested and home to the nomadic Oroqen people.

3. Yakutsk
A bitterly cold city for much of the year, this was a favoured place to send Russians into exile. Today, diamond mines have made Yakutsk a prosperous city.

4. Verkhoyansk
In 1933, a temperature of −68°C (−90°F) was recorded in this small Siberian town. This makes Verkhoyansk the world's coldest town.

5. Sakhalin Island
This island was once a haven for wildlife. Today, it is heavily industrialized and much of the forest has been removed.

6. Hokkaido
The forests of Hokkaido, the northern island of Japan, are home to Japanese macaques, the only monkeys to live in taiga.

7. Kuril Islands
The hundreds of desolate Kuril Islands hold great mineral resources. Russia and Japan are still arguing over who owns them.

8. Kamchatka
This mountainous region contains more than sixty active volcanoes. They form part of the Ring of Fire that encircles the Pacific Ocean.

China's forest nomads

Until the last 30 years, the Oroqen of northern China (right) lived a nomadic, hunting lifestyle similar to that of traditional Siberian forest dwellers. They herded reindeer, hunted deer and lived in tents covered with birch bark in summer and deer skins in winter. Today they live a more settled lifestyle, with modern conveniences such as radio and television. However, many still wear traditional clothes, including a hat made from a deer head, complete with antlers. This is worn by men when they hunt deer. Oroqen women continue to make household items and canoes from birch bark.

The future

Largely untamed, the taiga has escaped much of the impact of the modern world. However, tourism, industry and climate change all threaten to alter the biome in ways that we are only just beginning to understand.

The world appears to be warming up. In 2000, the International Panel on Climate Change (IPCC) calculated that world temperatures could rise by an average of 3°C (5.4°F) by the end of the 21st century. This would have many effects across the globe; for example, sea levels could rise by about 0.5 metres (20 in) – enough to flood many low-lying areas near the coast.

Greenhouse effect

Scientists believe that the cause of **global warming** is the build-up of **carbon dioxide** and other gases in the **atmosphere**. Carbon dioxide is released when fossil fuels, such as oil, coal and natural gas, are burned. Carbon dioxide is a greenhouse gas. It acts like glass in a greenhouse, trapping heat in the atmosphere and warming the planet's surface. Methane and water vapour are other greenhouse gases. Methane is released when dead material decays, and water vapour is added to the air when things are burnt.

An oil pipeline cuts through a taiga forest in Alaska. The pipe is held above the ground so that the oil it contains does not warm the ground and damage the permafrost.

Scientists believe that the taiga is one of the biomes most likely to change in size as a result of global warming. If the world warms, the taiga might shift many miles to the north within the next few centuries. As this happens, the bands of taiga forest around the world could also shrink in size.

If the taiga biome does get smaller, this may have an added effect on global warming. As trees grow, they take in carbon dioxide from the air during photosynthesis and turn it into sugar and wood. The sugar is the trees' fuel, and when it is used up, it is released back into the air as carbon dioxide. However, the carbon in the wood stays locked up in the tree until it eventually dies and decays.

When a new forest grows, it takes in more carbon dioxide than it gives out. If a forest is cut down and burned or left to decay, it releases all its carbon into the atmosphere. If global warming causes the taiga and other forest biomes to shrink in size, the overall number of trees will be reduced. The carbon in the trees that die away as the biomes shrink will be released into the atmosphere, making global warming even worse.

Within the taiga, the distribution of forest trees will alter as global warming increases. Mixed forests – containing both deciduous and coniferous trees – will probably become more widespread and extend further north, while the taiga as a whole gets smaller.

Sustainable use

Sustainable use means harvesting natural products at the same rate that they can replace themselves. In sustainable taiga forests, only a few trees are felled at a time. These are replaced by natural growth without the forest getting smaller overall.

57

A lumberjack cuts through the trunk of a massive tree on Vancouver Island, Canada, as part of a sustainable selective-logging operation.

One of the best ways to conserve forest is to establish protected reserves, in which the wood is harvested in sustainable ways. Instead of felling all the trees in an area – a practice known as clear-felling – lumberjacks are more selective in what trees they choose to remove. By leaving many trees in place and allowing younger trees to grow in the gaps, the soil is protected from erosion, and the forest floor keeps its cover of rare wild flowers, such as orchids.

Fire hazard

Fire plays an important natural role in the ecology of forests, helping to maintain a rich diversity of habitats by creating clearings. However, with global warming, fires might become too destructive. This may already be happening. Across the North American taiga, the area of forest that burned each year in the 1990s was about double that of the

 ## Protecting Russia's taiga

The Pechoro-Ilychskiy Reserve lies on the western slopes of the Ural Mountains in Russia. It was set up to protect areas of taiga, tundra and alpine meadow. Its taiga regions include lowland pine forest, sphagnum bog and foothills of dark taiga (fir and spruce).

Set up in 1930, the reserve was reduced to about 10 per cent of its original size in the 1950s, but was enlarged again, in 1959, to about 60 per cent of its original size. Between the 1950s and 1980s, some of the forests were cut down and the elk and reindeer, which had been protected, were hunted once again.

In 1984, the wildlife park was given international biosphere reserve status, providing greater protection. It remains an important place for animals and plants

that are typical inhabitants of the European and Asian taiga. More than 500 species of flowering plants and 40 species of mammals, including brown bears, wolverines, pine martens, sable, red squirrels, chipmunks and beavers, live in the park. It also harbours 200 species of birds and at least 17 types of fish.

Botanists and zoologists have studied the ups and downs of the resident populations over long periods. In the 1950s, the world's first elk farm was set up in the reserve. Scientific studies here make this among the world's best sources of information on elk behaviour. The greatest threat to the reserve is not pollution but changes in government policy that could allow more development in the area.

Pollution problems

When fossil fuels burn, they release chemicals that can cause acid rain. These chemicals – oxides of sulphur and nitrogen – can drift north from Europe, Asia and the USA, producing acid rain in the taiga.

Acid rain damages trees directly (below right), scorching leaves, stripping them of their protective waxy coating. The leaves' pores are blocked by salts produced by the acids, so that trees can no longer photosynthesize efficiently. The acid can also release harmful metals locked in the soil, killing tree roots and affecting soil microbes. Overall, this weakens trees, making them more vulnerable to attacks by pests. Some trees are more susceptible to acid rain than others, so pollution can change the composition of forests.

Acid rain has another effect. It washes dissolved metals, such as aluminium, from the soil. These metals enter the taiga's lakes and rivers. The chemicals may kill all life and stop dead material from decomposing.

Pulp and paper mills and ore smelters can produce serious heavy-metal poisoning of rivers. Many rivers in the Siberian taiga are spectacularly polluted. For example, in the 1990s, cellulose-processing factories on the banks of the Amur River, which is near the border with China, discharged more than 38,000 million litres (10,000 million gallons) of polluted waste into the river every year. Close to these outlets, all young fish are killed, including those of valuable commercial species.

1940s. If this trend continues, the benefits of fire will soon be outweighed by the damage it causes to forests.

Forest fires add carbon dioxide to the atmosphere, perhaps increasing the greenhouse effect and speeding up global warming. If there are more fires in the future, the tree composition of the forests will change. The trees that are good at resisting fire will become more common, as will plants that grow quickly from seed after fire has passed.

The spread of agriculture

Taiga country is not good for growing crops and raising livestock, such as cattle. Taiga people raise reindeer inside the thick forests, since the deer can manage to exist by eating lichens, snow-buried berries and mushrooms in the depths of winter. Cattle cannot survive the harsh winters, however, without fodder, such as hay, being given to them.

Despite the difficulties of raising crops in the harsh climate and thin soil of the taiga, growing cereals and vegetables has been a tradition among some taiga peoples in North America, Europe and Asia. Wheat and rye for bread-making, and vegetables such as carrots and turnips, make a welcome addition to their diet of meat and fish. Nevertheless, forest clearance for these crops has had fairly little impact on the taiga as a whole. Of much greater impact is farming at the southern edge of the taiga.

A salmon fisherman shows off his catch in a river in eastern Canada. Tourism and leisure are growing industries in taiga forests.

The southern limits of the taiga are being pushed further north, as forests are cleared for growing crops and rearing cattle. In central Canada, for example, farmers combine cattle-rearing with growing cereal crops as cattle feed. The cattle graze on grasses sown under thin forests of deciduous taiga trees, such as quaking aspen and poplar. In British Columbia and Alberta, farmers grow cereals, oilseed rape for vegetable oils and plants to feed their cattle.

In the milder areas of southern Ontario and Quebec, clover, corn and potatoes are the favoured crops. As the human populations of North America and Russia rise, the desire to clear land along the southern edges of the taiga for use as farms grows ever stronger.

Canada's protected forests

There are two taiga reserves in Canada – Riding Mountain in Manitoba and Charlevoix in Quebec. The Charlevoix Reserve (below) contains fir, spruce, pine and maple forest in the lowlands as well as mountain taiga. An important part of the reserve is the wetland drained by the St Lawrence River and its tributaries.

Among the reserve's largest animals are the lynx, beaver, caribou (reindeer) and blue snow goose. In the 1960s, caribou were re-introduced to the area. They had been cleared from the forests by hunting many decades before. The reserve is now a popular tourist destination, with nature trails and with local scientists working to educate the public.

Riding Mountain National Park is an island of taiga forest surrounded by the prairies and wetlands of Manitoba. Riding Mountain is the highest point on the Manitoba Escarpment, which forms the centrepiece of the park.

Although it is a small park compared to North America's other reserves of taiga, Riding Mountain does not lack wildlife. In addition to wolves, black bears and moose, the park is home to the largest herd of wood bison in the world. These animals are very rare and found only in the southern edges of North American taiga. However, the park animals are still at risk from hunters. Black bears and deer are lured out of the park with baits, where they are shot for sport. Bear hunting is legal in Canada, but shooting deer is not.

Managing the taiga

Like many wilderness areas around the world, the taiga is being scoured for reserves of fossil fuels. The mountain rivers in the biome are also tapped for their energy. In Canada, for example, dams in the taiga provide 60 per cent of the country's electricity. All this activity is changing the face of the taiga. Dams flood huge areas of forest, while trees cleared by oil workers in the far north of the taiga cannot grow back because the permafrost layer rises to the surface.

With or without global warming, the taiga will come under increasing pressure. As things stand, taiga forests may have been cut back by 50 per cent or more, along with temperate and tropical forests, since people first began to fell trees. Scientists and foresters understand the simpler ecology of taiga forests better than the more fertile and complex forests to the south. This is a good starting point for the scientists, industrialists and governments who work together to find ways to manage the taiga in a more sustainable way.

It is difficult, if not impossible, to put a value on the world's taiga forests. Their value lies not just in the wood they contain, or their ability to clean the air, stop flooding or provide a living for millions of people. The forests, and the animals and plants within them, have a priceless beauty of their own.

Some scientists suggest that planting more fast-growing taiga trees might slow or even stop global warming by absorbing extra carbon dioxide from the air. Unfortunately, the calculations do not add up. Much more forest would need to be planted than there is suitable space to do so. The best way to beat global warming is for governments to reduce the amount of fuels being burned, and to build flood defences against rising sea levels.

In the meantime, the taiga forests continue to flourish. Whatever the future holds, they are likely to last for many years to come, providing we keep a watchful eye on them.

This dam across a river in Canadian taiga converts the water's energy into electricity. The power is used by towns and cities far from the taiga.

Glossary

alga (plural algae) simple, plant-like organism that makes food from sunlight

Algonquian family of Native American languages spoken by people in eastern Canada and the eastern USA

Athabascan family of Native American languages spoken by people in western Canada

Arctic Circle imaginary line drawn around the North Pole on which there is midnight sun for one day in midsummer

atmosphere layer of air around the Earth

bacterium (plural bacteria) single-celled micro-organism; among the simplest forms of life

biome major division of the living world, distinguished by its climate and wildlife. Tundra, desert and temperate grasslands are examples of biomes.

bog type of wetland in which partly decayed plant matter builds up in soggy, acidic ground

canopy layer formed at the top of a forest by branches and leaves. Some shrublands have a broken canopy formed by shrubs.

carbon dioxide gas released when fuel burns. Carbon dioxide is one of the main gases thought to cause global warming.

climate pattern of weather that happens in one place during an average year

conifer type of plant that does not have true fruit like flowering plants but instead produces seeds protected inside a cone

deciduous plant that sheds all its leaves every year

desert place that receives less than 250 mm (10 in) of rain a year

dormant so inactive as to appear lifeless. Plant seeds often stay dormant until their soil gets wet.

ecosystem collection of living animals and plants that function together with their environment

equator imaginary line around the Earth, midway between the North and South Poles

erosion gradual wearing away of land by the action of wind, rain, rivers, ice or the sea

evaporate to turn into gas. When water evaporates, it becomes an invisible part of the air.

evergreen plant that keeps its leaves all year round

fertile capable of sustaining plant growth

fungus (plural fungi) type of organism, neither plant nor animal, that gets its food by digesting plant or animal material, living or dead

geyser jet of hot water or steam produced by volcanic activity

glacier river of ice that flows slowly off a mountain or ice sheet

global warming gradual warming of the Earth's climate, thought to be caused by pollution of the atmosphere

hemisphere one half of the Earth. The northern hemisphere is the half to the north of the equator.

hibernation time of dormancy that some animals go through during winter

hypha (plural hyphae) thin fibres of a fungus, usually growing underground

ice age period when the Earth's climate was cooler and the polar ice caps expanded. The last ice age ended 10,000 years ago.

lichen partnership between algae and fungi

mammal warm-blooded animal that feeds its young on milk

migration long-distance journey by an animal to find food or a breeding site

mycorrhiza (plural mycorrhizae) fungus that is lives in partnership with a plant's roots

nomad person who travels from place to place in search of food and water

nutrient any chemical that nourishes plants or animals, helping them grow

oxygen gas in the air. Animals and plants need to take in oxygen so that their cells can release energy from food.

peat partly decayed dead plant matter that builds up in bogs

permafrost permanently frozen ground under the surface of some taiga

photosynthesis chemical process that plants and algae use to make food from simple chemicals and the sun's energy

pollen dust-like powder produced by the male parts of flowers

pollination transfer of pollen from the male part of a flower to the female part of the same flower or another flower, causing the flower to produce seeds

prairie large area of grassland in central North America

predator animal that catches and eats other animals

protein one of the major food groups. It is used for building and repairing plant and animal bodies.

rainforest lush forest that receives frequent heavy rainfall

rain shadow area where rainfall is low because nearby mountains provide shelter from rain-bearing winds

species particular type of organism. Cheetahs are a species, for instance, but birds are not, because there are lots of different bird species.

temperate having a moderate climate. The temperate zone lies between the warm, tropical regions and the cold, polar regions.

temperate forest biome that mainly contains broad-leaved trees. Temperate forests grow the the south of most areas of taiga.

tropical within about 2575 km (1600 miles) of the equator

tropical forest forest in the Earth's tropical zone, such as tropical rainforest or monsoon forest

tropical grassland tropical biome in which grass is the main form of plant life

tundra biome of the far north, made up of treeless plains covered with small plants. Tundra begins at the northern edge of taiga forests.

water vapour water in gas form

Further research

Books

Farndon, John. *The Wildlife Atlas*. London: Marshall Editions, 2002.
Henry, J. David. *Canada's Boreal Forest*. Washington, D.C.: Smithsonian Institution Press, 2002.
Johnson, Rebecca. *A Walk in the Boreal Forest*. Minneapolis: Carolrhoda Books, 2001.
London, Jack. *Call of the Wild*. London: Puffin Books, 1994.
(The famous adventure novel about a dog during the Klondike Gold Rush, which took place in the taiga forest of Canada and Alaska around a hundred years ago.)
Kaplan, Elizabeth. *Taiga: Biomes of the World*. New York: Benchmark Books, 1996.

Websites

The Boreal Forest Network: www.borealnet.org/main.html
(Information about North American taiga forests.)
World Wildlife Fund Ecoregions: www.worldwildlife.org/wildworld/profiles/terrestrial_pa.html
(Learn about the world's ecoregions, including the Siberian boreal forest.)
Taiga Rescue Network Photo Gallery: www.taigarescue.org/photo_gallery/photo_gallery.php
(Pictures of taiga forests around the world.)

Index

Picture credits

Key: l – left, r – right, m – middle, t – top, b – bottom. **Ardea:** Avon Dennis 41; John Cancalosi 51; Francois Gohier 26; Arthur Hayward 31 (inset); Chris Knights 17; Stefan Mayers 42r; J. E. Swedberg 16, 60t; Zdenek Tunka 37; Art Explosion: 36b; **Bruce Coleman:** Natural Selection Inc. 11 (inset), 12; **Corbis:** Yann Arthus-Bertrand 60b; Joel Bennett 48t; Bettmann 53b; Dean Conger 46; Richard A. Cooke 50; Alissa Crandall 9; Wolfgang Kaehler 7m, 7r, 44, 45, 54; Layne Kennedy 53t; Earl and Nazima Kowall 55; Joe McDonald 32; Neil Rabinowitz 48b; Paul A. Souders 49, 56; Karen Tweedy-Holmes 19; Kennan Ward 42l; **Digital Stock:** World Panoramas 7l, 30/31; **Image Bank:** J. H. Pete Carmichael 28; Steve Niedorf Photography 6r, 18; Paul Stover 22; Art Wolfe 6m, 8; **NHPA:** B. and C. Alexander 47; Henry Ausloos 34; Laurie Campbell 21; Robert Erwin 25; Paal Hermansen 10, 24, 59; Karl Switak 14; T. Kitchin and V. Hurst 35, 39, 58; **Oxford Scientific Films:** Paul Taylor 36t; **Photodisc:** Geostock 61; Robert Glusic 4m; Bruce Heinemann 5l; Jack Hollingsworth 5m; PhotoLink 5r, 13, 23, 29, 38, 52; Karl Weatherley 4r, 20; Jeremy Woodhouse 33. **Title page:** Photodisc, Jeremy Woodhouse. **Front cover:** NHPA, Karl Switak and Henry Ausloos (inset).